WINNING
THE BATTLE OF
THE MIND

GREGORY DICKOW

Winning the Battle of the Mind
©2003 by Gregory Dickow Ministries.

All rights reserved.

Unless otherwise noted, all Scripture quotations in this
volume are from the King James Version of the Bible.

Scripture quotations marked (AMP) are taken from the
Amplified Bible, Copyright © 1954, 1958, 1962, 1964, 1965,
1987 by The Lockman Foundation.
Used by permission.

Printed in the United States of America

For information, please write
Gregory Dickow Ministries,
P.O. Box 7000
Chicago, IL 60680

or visit us online at www.changinglives.org.

TABLE OF CONTENTS

WINNING THE BATTLE OF THE MIND

~≈~

Introduction

"Finally my brethren, be strong in the Lord and in the power of his might. Put on the whole armor of God that you may be able to stand against the wiles of the devil" (Ephesians 6:10-11).

What does that mean—"the wiles of the devil?" Do you remember the Road Runner?

The Road Runner used to be chased by the coyote, right? And the coyote had a first name and a middle name. It was Wile E. Coyote, right? He was a wily coyote. In other words, he was a coyote that was always coming up with wiles, which means schemes. He would have a scheme, a strategy or a plot to trap the Road Runner so he could eat him up. I don't know why he would want to eat him because the Road Runner had no meat on his bones, and he had a nasty attitude!

Now I actually saw this. I was in California once at a meeting and somebody took me to this church that was on a hill and I literally saw a road runner run across the parking lot. Within a minute or two, along came a coyote following after him. All of the sudden I realized—this cartoon is real! Remember that song? "That coyote is really a crazy clown. When will he learn that he never can pull him down? Poor little Road Runner never bothers anyone... Road Runner, the Coyote's after you. Road Runner, if he catches you you're through."

Allow me to put this in Biblical perspective (if I can)! How does this relate to us? "Finally my brethren, put on the whole armor of God that you may be able to stand against the wiles of the devil." Now I'll give you some big "sophisticated" Greek words to make up for all the silly words that I've already used so you'll know that I don't just think in cartoons and songs, although it helps.

The word "wiles" in this verse could be translated as "schemes" or "methods." The word "wile" comes from a Greek word *"methodos,"* which means the devil has a method or a roadway to get into our lives. We get the word "road" from the second part of this Greek word, *"odos."* So when he says that the devil has a "wile" or a method, what he literally means is: the devil has a method of building a road into your life so that once he gets access through that road, he can influence the outcome of your life.

As the scripture continues, God tells us to *"put on the whole armor of God that we may be able to stand against the wiles of the devil."* So the devil has a scheme or a method to build a road and gain access into our lives. What is that road? As we will see throughout this book—it is our thought life! Our thought life is the road Satan uses to drive into our finances, our marriage, our health, and every other area of our lives. As we win the battle of our mind, we will experience the true freedom and power that we all long for.

We're going to see in the Word of God that Satan doesn't have authority in our lives, but he creates thoughts and lies so that once those thoughts get into our head, it paves the way, or it paves the road for his influence. Let's first understand, however, that Jesus already defeated the devil 2,000 years ago…

JESUS DEFEATED THE DEVIL

~~~

Chapter One

For this purpose the Son of God was manifested that He might destroy the works of the devil" (1 John 3:8).

Jesus' purpose for coming to this earth was to destroy the works of the devil—and He did not fail in that purpose! The devil's real power was destroyed 2,000 years ago.

The devil does not have the power in our lives that many Christians think he has. We need to understand that. The devil does not have power to destroy your home. The devil does not have power to destroy your marriage. The devil does not have the power to destroy your body or your physical health. The devil does not have the power to destroy your finances. The devil doesn't have any of that power. But what the devil does have is the power to **tell you lies.** It's the lies of the devil that have the power to destroy your marriage, your home, your finances, your emotions, your children, your family or anything else in your life. It is his lies that must be exposed and rejected.

He has been defeated. He has been vanquished. Satan has been stripped of all of his authority. Remember, Satan received his authority in this earth from Adam. He didn't receive it from God. God gave authority in this life to Adam. Adam gave his authority to the devil when Adam and Eve bowed their knee to Satan. They committed high treason against God. When Adam and Eve refused to obey God, and instead obeyed what the devil told them, then Satan became their lord. And when Satan became their lord, Satan possessed the authority that Adam and Eve had been entrusted with by God. Satan now had authority over Adam and Eve, over the earth, and over everything that God had given to man.

That is why Jesus came—to take back that authority from Satan—which he successfully did 2,000 years ago. After Jesus died and rose from the dead, He said, *"Now I hold the keys of Hell and death. All authority has been given to Me in Heaven and in earth and under the earth and now I give you authority."* He said, *"Now I give you authority"* (Revelation 1:18; Matthew 28:18; Luke 10:19).

So here's how it went down: God gave authority to Adam and Eve. Adam and Eve gave that authority to the devil when they sinned. Jesus came to the earth and took that authority back from the devil and He gave that authority to us.

The Bible says we are now seated with Christ in heavenly places, ruling and reigning with Him as He shares with us the authority and power that He walks in.

Ephesians 2:5-6 says, *"Even when we were dead in sins, hath quickened us together with Christ, (by grace ye are saved;) And hath raised us up together, and made us sit together in heavenly places in Christ Jesus."*

We now have the capacity to walk in the same level of power that Jesus walked in, because we are joined to Him. Romans 8:16

says, *"We are joint heirs with Jesus Christ, and heirs of this world."* The sooner we understand that, the sooner we will get a hold of the fact that we are not little humans that don't have any power; puppets for the devil; as soon as we understand that we are not under the power of the devil, the sooner we will take our rightful place as sons and daughters of God, and win the battle of the mind.

Isaiah 54:17 declares, *"No weapon formed against you shall prosper."* Psalm 91:10 declares, *"No evil shall befall you, nor any plague or calamity come near your tent."* In Luke 10:19 Jesus says to us, *"Behold I give you authority to trample upon serpents and scorpions and over all the power of the enemy and nothing shall by any means injure, hurt, or harm you."* That's power. That's authority! Yes, the devil has already been defeated. Believe it. Accept it. Now let's move on.

THE WILES OF
THE ENEMY

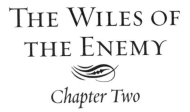

Chapter Two

Now, although Satan has lost his authority and power over your life, he does have a method of operating that I want to show you so you will win the battle of your mind.

The gospel is the power of God, but we need to learn how to walk in that power and we need to learn how Satan operates. I don't want to give the devil a lot of attention, but I want us to understand how he operates, so we can resist his operation in our lives since he has no legal authority over us.

Remember when the devil came to God about Job and said, "If you curse Job then he'll curse you." And the Lord said, "He's under your power, Satan." He's basically saying, "He's not under my power, he's under your power because he's not saved." You see, when you're not born again, you're under the power of the devil. But when you get born again, you are no longer under the power of the devil. You are under the power of God, and you now have power over the devil.

So when Satan comes along, you need to understand you have authority over him. But how does he operate so we can accurately exercise our authority?

Let's look again at Ephesians 6:11. *"Put on the whole armor of God that you may be able to stand against the wiles of the devil."*

Let me try to make more sense out of that by defining for you the word, "devil." The word devil comes from the Greek word *"diabalos."* Our Spanish-speaking readers understand the word for devil is *diablo.* This Greek word is broken down into two words, *"dia"* and *"balos."*

Starting with the second word, *"balos,"* it means "to throw at." It's where we get the word "ball" from. It means "to throw or to hurl accusations at." It means "to throw accusations, negative words or negative thoughts at."

The word *"dia"* is where we get the word "diameter" from, which means "to put a hole through or penetrate."

If we put these two words together—*"dia"* which means "to penetrate," and *"balos"* which means "to throw at," then we understand the way the devil operates. His whole method is to throw accusations at you over and over and over and over and over again until he penetrates your mind, and once you give in, he releases his explosive power into your life. He is *"dia-balos,"* the accuser who will keep accusing until he penetrates your thought life. Satan doesn't have any other method. He can't send demons to defeat you. He can't send strongholds to destroy you. He can't send principalities to be principal over you. He can't do any of that because that's not how he operates.

His method or his scheme—his roadway into your life is through your thoughts.

The good news about that is that we can seal him off and recognize his one point of entry into our lives—primarily through our thought life. So when we get control of that one point of entry then we leave him no more access. In America, there are many points of entry. There is the Atlantic Ocean, the Pacific Ocean, Canada, and Mexico.

In our lives, however, there is only one point of entry. So in America, it's very difficult sometimes to control every point of access. If we were able to reduce the points of entry into our country to one, then we would have much better control.

In the same way, we need to understand that the devil has only one point of entry into our lives—our thought life. We can certainly control our life and what we allow into our life a whole lot better when we understand that one point of access.

That is why the Bible says, "Do not be conformed to this world but be transformed by the renewing of your mind."

As you're transformed by the renewing of your mind—as you renew your mind to the Word of God—as you wash your thought life to agree with the Word of God, you are eliminating Satan's access into your life.

Satan has no legal right or authority over you. You have authority over him. So he tries to piggy-back on thoughts that will defeat us. He's like a train robber who jumps onto a moving train and gets inside the train. He jumps on the train and gets access into the cabins. Then he can do whatever he wants to do to the people on that train. That's what Satan wants to do. He wants to piggy-back on the train of your thought life and thereby gain access in your life and release his explosive power.

Let's find out now, how to close this entry point into our lives—stop him—and stop the train wreck!

WHERE THE BATTLE REALLY IS

Chapter Three

Remember, the coyote is after you. But he's been defeated and now we know where he gains access so we can seal him off. It's really simple. The Christian life is not as hard as we try to make it. It's really a battle going on in your mind and it's a war going on between your ears. It's not a battle against devils and demons. It's a battle against their thoughts.

Nowhere does the Bible say to take every demon captive, but as I'm about to show you, the Bible does say, "Take every thought captive." I'm not saying that you shouldn't cast out devils. You should cast out devils, but we cast devils out of demon-possessed people. If you're born again, you're a "Jesus-possessed" person not a "demon-possessed" person. You might have ways of behaving that are due to a system of thinking that needs to be taken captive. So when you destroy that system of thinking, your behavior will change.

You cannot change your life by changing your behavior. You change your life by changing how you think. When your thinking lines up with God's thinking, then Satan cannot get in. He's sealed off. He cannot penetrate your life. He will come and he will try to penetrate. Remember, he is *diabalos.* He is going to throw accusations at you, and throw accusations at you, and throw accusations at you until he penetrates and then releases his explosive power. But if he can't penetrate because you have your shield of faith up, if he can't penetrate because you have your breastplate of righteousness on, if he can't penetrate because you have your sword of the Spirit out, then he will have no success against you!

Have you ever met someone who you thought, "Oh man, they're a Christian but why do they act that way? Why are they weird? Why are they strange? Why do I not want to get near that person?" It is because that person carries an attitude and carries a spirit about him that is built by a system of thinking developed in his life.

I believe in deliverance, and I believe you can come up and we can pray and we can break the power of certain forces in your life, but you are going to have to change your system of thinking or you're going to be back up in the same prayer line with the same problem. If you smoke, and you come up in the prayer line, we can pray for you to be healed from cancer, but if you keep acting like the Marlboro Man outside of church then that cancer has plenty of access back into your life. In the same way, we can cast the devil out of you, we can bind the devil, we can pull down the strongholds and bind the principalities, but I'm telling you if we don't change our system of thinking, then Satan will have the same access back into our lives that he had the first time.

When you were a sinner, Satan owned you. Because he owned you, he infiltrated your life with ways of thinking that were land mines to produce destruction along the course of your life. Once you get born again, he no longer has authority over you, but he still has a system of thinking that he has placed inside of your head through this world's system and we need to break down that system of thinking so that it is no longer our way of thinking and therefore can no longer do damage.

That's what the Word of God is for—to change our way of thinking. It's to give us a new way of thinking so that we are no longer paving the way for Satan to have access into our lives.

Proverbs 23:6-8 says, *"Do not eat the bread of him that has an evil eye neither desire his dainty meats. For as he thinks in his heart, so is he. Eat and drink he says to you but his heart is not with you."* The devil understands this verse. He cannot do anything to you unless your mind and your flesh cooperate with him. Notice the context in which God is saying,

"As a man thinks, so is he." He's saying that a person can pay you compliments. A person can invite you to dinner. A person can say, "Eat and drink, you're welcome here." But just because they say that, it does not reveal who they really are. ***Who they really are is what they're thinking on the inside.***

We have been told that we are what we say, but we need to understand something—***what we think is who we really are.*** What we're really thinking on the inside is who we really are. Someone may ask you, "How are you doing?" And you're thinking, "Man, I'm lousy. I feel bad. I don't feel good." And you say, "Everything is fine."

You may be saying "everything is fine," thinking you're making a faith statement, but what I'm telling you is: who you really are is made up of what you are thinking inside. As you think within, that's who you really are, and that's why we have to pay more attention to changing the thoughts that we think even more than changing the words that we speak.

We can be saying things that we don't really believe and no matter how often we say those things, if we don't really believe, they are not going to have power. That's why so many Christians are discouraged with the concept of speaking the Word or confessing the Word.

I am an advocate of speaking the Word of God out of our mouths, but I am not an advocate of speaking the Word of God that you don't really believe in your heart. And that's why he says, "If you believe in your heart and say with your mouth, 'Jesus is Lord' then you'll be saved." Salvation is a by-product of the words that we speak that are in alignment and agreement with what we believe in our heart. So the focus needs to be on what we believe or what we're thinking.

The focus can't be merely on just what we say. Look at Mark 11:23. It has been often quoted as: "Say to this mountain, 'Be thou removed and cast into the sea,' and it shall obey." *But It doesn't say that.* It says:

*"Whosoever shall say to this mountain, 'Be thou removed and cast into the sea,' **and believes in his heart** or shall not doubt in his heart that those things which he says shall happen, he shall have whatsoever he says."*

We see it as *"Those things that he says shall be granted to him,"* but we are missing the most important step, and that is **believing it in our heart.** The reason we don't believe it in our heart is because we're trying to conduct ourselves in appropriate Christian manner, which is to say right things, to speak the Word; and that is proper conduct. But if we don't deal with our thought life, our conduct of confession will not produce any results.

Do you see why there are so many Christians that have spoken the Word, but they haven't seen anything change? That thing is only going to change based on the weight of confidence in your heart that you actually have—not just the words that you actually speak. It takes both of those working together. What you believe and what you think needs to precede what you say. When you say what you really believe and what you really are thinking, that's when your words have power.

But when the things you say out of your mouth are not in alignment with what you really think in your heart, your words are not going to have any power. And that's why we're often discouraged. We have tried confessing the

Word, but we have not focused on our thought life, which is where our creative power is.

Our thought life is the author or the parent of what we believe in our heart. What we believe in our heart, when spoken out, is going to come to pass; but when we speak something that we don't really believe in our heart, it won't have any power.

You may say, "Is that really true?" Well, think about it in your own life. Think about all the things that you really didn't believe but you said them out of your mouth anyway because you thought this "confession stuff" should work. It really didn't change anything because you didn't have the confidence in your heart to back up the words that came out of your mouth.

It's critical those two things work together and that disconnect is why things aren't working. I'm not an engineer or an electrician, but if we plug something into a power outlet that is not connected to the power plant, nothing is going to happen. It may look like an electric outlet—it may look like a power source—but if it's disconnected behind the scenes, it is not going to produce any results.

In the same way, you might speak words that may look like you're confessing the Word but if there's nothing behind the scenes, if you're disconnected behind the scenes, it's not going to change anything. That's why we've got to deal with what is behind the scenes. That's where our emphasis ought to be: in our thought life. That's where we ought to be changing things. Then our confession is going to come out of the overflow of our heart—out of the overflow of what we really believe and what we really think. That's when things will change on the outside! As a man thinks within, so is he.

That ought to set us free. That ought to make us skip like a kid and run like a deer. It ought to make us so free. Why? Because now I know what I need to focus on—what I'm thinking. *My thought life is the road by which Satan gets access into my life and my thought life is the road by which God gets access into my life.* And so I need to make sure I have some police officers patrolling that road.

That's why it's so important that we deal with our thought life as Christians. So we need to get control of our thought life; do some construction around those roads that are influencing our lives and make sure that our thoughts create a way for God to have access into our life, not the devil.

How to Win the Battle

Chapter Four

God is a results God. When He plants a seed He expects a harvest. When He sent His Son to this earth He expected many sons. He wants us to have results as well, and share the glory of experiencing the manifestation of our prayers.

This answers the question, "Why aren't my prayers working?" Because a prayer uttered in desperation, without the thought life backing it up, will not produce any change in that situation. Elijah was able to say to the weather, "You're not going to rain for three and a half years," because he really believed that. That's why it didn't rain for three and a half years.

Why were the disciples drowning when the storm was in their boat, while Jesus was able to say, "Peace, be still," and the storm stopped? Let me tell you why. Jesus is the

Prince of Peace and on the inside of Him He had an image of peace. So when He said to the storm, "Peace, be still," He was bringing forth from the peace that was within Him and making that circumstance line up with what was on the inside of Him already. He wasn't disturbed on the inside. "Peace" had power to come to pass because peace was born out of what was already in Him.

The peace of God must rule in your heart, first. *"Let the peace of Christ rule in your heart,"*

Colossians 3:15 tells us. Philippians 4:6 says, *"Be anxious for nothing but in everything with prayer and petition, with thanksgiving, let your requests be made known to God and the peace which surpasses all comprehension shall guard your heart."* It won't guard your circumstance until it first guards your heart. It won't deal with your situation until it first has dealt with your heart. That's why Jesus said, "Let not your heart be troubled." He is saying, "When your heart is troubled, then everything around you is going to be troubled." Though you may have trouble all around you, whatever is in your heart (your thought life) will eventually come out and bring peace to the trouble in your life.

But if your heart is troubled, then you can't change the situation since the trouble in your life is also in your heart. There has to be something bigger in your heart than what's in your life, so it can change your life.

TAKING THOUGHTS CAPTIVE

Chapter Five

"For though we walk in the flesh we do not war after the flesh for the weapons of our warfare are not carnal but mighty through God to the pulling down of strongholds, casting down imaginations and every high thing that exalts itself against the knowledge

*of God and **bringing into captivity
every thought to the obedience
of Christ"** (2 Corinthians 10:3-5).*

Now he mentions three things here in these verses. He says, "strongholds, imaginations, and thoughts." A thought, unchecked, will become an imagination. And when we say "imagination" we can break that word down and say "image." A thought is going to produce an image.

When I say the word "dog" to you, you don't see the letters, d-o-g. When I say the word "dog" to you, what do you see? You see your Chihuahua. You see your Golden Retriever, or whatever kind of dog you have. That's what you see. You see a picture. When the devil says, "failure" you see a picture. When the devil says "sickness" you see a picture. Maybe you see a funeral. Maybe you see a hospital bed. Maybe you see yourself dying and falling apart. When the devil speaks a thought into your mind, it creates a picture. When that thought is meditated on, over time it creates a vivid picture, and that imagination becomes a stronghold. What is a stronghold? It's something that has a "strong" "hold" over you. So it starts as a thought, then it grows into an image, and that's when it becomes a stronghold.

So if we want to tear down strongholds, we've got to deal with our imaginations or our images. And if we want to deal with the images we have to deal with our thought life.

Though we can portray a godly, Christian life on the outside, we've got to deal with our thought life on the inside, because that's who we really are. That is what's really going to manifest in our lives. This is why our thoughts must be on what God thinks about us. We've got to develop the right image or imagination on the inside. We must understand the image of who we really are on the inside and then meditate on that image. That image is going to give us a "strong hold" over whatever the devil is trying to do in our life, rather than it having a strong hold over us.

"…Bringing into captivity every thought to the obedience of Christ." That word "captivity"

has two words attached to it in Greek. It has the word "sword" and it has the word "conquer." So to conquer with a sword is what this word means: to take captive. When He says we need to bring into "captivity" every thought, He's saying, "The way to bring every thought into captivity is to conquer your thoughts with a sword." The only thing that can conquer your thoughts is a sword.

Well, it just so happens that one of the pieces of armor that God has given us is called "the sword of the Spirit" which is "the Word of God," according to Ephesians 6:17.

So the only way to take a thought captive or to conquer it with a sword, is to conquer every thought with the sword of the Spirit, which is the Word of God. The only way to take a thought captive is to attack it with something greater than it, and what is greater than a thought? The Word of God. What is greater than the thought of sickness? The Word of God. What is greater than the thought of disease? The

Word of God. What is greater than the thought of failure? The Word of God. What is greater than the thought of your family falling apart? The Word of God. In other words, the Word of God is greater than any thought. So as you think and speak the Word, the sword of the Spirit conquers every contrary thought.

THE IMAGE OF GOD IN YOU

Chapter Six

Let me illustrate this a little differently so that you get this picture in your mind. I want you to see that your mind is the road that Satan uses to get access in your life. Let's say that our life is an office building. You know how some companies have a receptionist that checks everybody before they go in. Sometimes the receptionist is mean and demanding. If you don't know the maiden name of the boss' mother's father's uncle's brother's sister, you're not going to get through because she is going to say, "Do you have an appointment?" "No, not really." "Do you know anybody here?" "Well, not really." "Well, did you talk to anybody?"

That receptionist is going to take control. She is going to be the gatekeeper of who is allowed into that office. Now I want you to see your life like that office building, and I want you to put a gatekeeper in your mind. I want you to see there's a receptionist that every thought has to check in with first.

When you go to an office, you have to check in or you go to a place where you have to register. Some complexes have a little circular area in the middle of the lobby and you have to check in there before you can get in. You give your name and that's when they start to question you. That's a good thing. You need to act that way. You need to have a circular desk in your head and in your heart that says, "I've got a receptionist here that every thought has to check in with first and then my receptionist is going to determine whether we're going to let you into our life or not."

Who is that receptionist? What is that gatekeeper inside of our mind that should be controlling every thought and that thought should have to check in with? It's the image of God on the inside of you. *The image of God on the inside of you must be the gatekeeper of every thought that comes into your life.*

Here is how it works. A thought of sickness comes against you and comes to knock on your door saying, "I'd like to come in and begin to possess your body, and control your body, and begin to take over little cells in your body, and my name is cancer." Well, the image of God needs to say, "Whoa, whoa whoa! Wait one minute there little buddy. I am sorry. But you don't pass the test. You don't look like the image of God to me. Therefore you're going to have to take your little behind out of my office, off of my desk, out of my building and get thee behind me, Satan!"

Every thought has to check in with the image of God. Some thoughts of poverty and some thoughts of lack begin to come against you. You need to say, "Whoa, wait a minute. Let me check the image of God." The image of God says, "No. We don't have that in our image." The image of God does not include lack. The image of God does not include poverty. The image of God does not include insufficiency. So we just will not allow that thought into our life.

Everything has got to check in at the registration desk. And if it does not have the mark of the image of God, it's not allowed in the building. If it does not have the mark of the image of God, it's not allowed in your life.

Let's talk about mountains in our lives for a moment. The reason why you should be able to speak to any mountain and command it to be removed is because you have an image on the inside of you that's bigger than the mountain. We can't see ourselves as "little" people trying to speak to "big" mountains. We have to see ourselves as big people looking down at a little mountain, and knocking it over like an ant hill. The mountains in our lives need to look like an ant hill because we have an image on the inside of us that's greater and bigger than anything. We are made in the image of God! What mountain is bigger than Him?

1 John 4:4 says, *"Greater is He that's in me than he that's in the world."* That's the image you have to have of yourself. That's the picture you have to have of yourself. How do you get that picture? You look into the mirror of God's Word and get the image of who you really look like. 1 John 4:18 says just as He is, so are we! God's Word says you look just like Jesus, and that image has to be the registration desk that every thought has to check in with.

The Word of God is our mirror, reflecting the image of who we really are and what we are to think. 2 Corinthians 3:18 says,

"But we all with unveiled face, beholding as in a mirror, the glory of the Lord, are constantly being transfigured into His very own image in ever increasing splendor and from one degree of glory to another..."

Keep looking, keep thinking in agreement with this picture. Keep seeing yourself exactly as the Word says you are and you will win the battle of the mind. You will conquer your thought life. You will cut off the devil's access into your life and you will experience the victorious and fulfilling life that Jesus promised you can have.

"... But I have come that you might have life and enjoy life, and have it in abundance to the full, until it overflows" *(John 10:10 AMP).*

About the Author

Gregory Dickow is the host of "The Power to Change Today," a dynamic television show seen throughout the world, reaching a potential half a billion households. He is also the founder and Senior Pastor of Life Changers International Church, a diverse and thriving congregation in the Chicago area with several thousand in weekly attendance.

Known for his ability to communicate the power and principles of God's Word clearly and concisely, Pastor Dickow lives to see the lives of people dramatically changed forever.

Pastor Dickow is also the host of "Ask the Pastor" a live radio show reaching the world through radio and the internet with live callers asking real questions about their real problems. Pastor Dickow is reaching people personally, encouraging them and empowering them to succeed in every area of life.

Other Books Available by Pastor Gregory Dickow

- Acquiring Beauty
- Breaking the Power of Inferiority
- Conquering Your Flesh
- Financial Freedom
- How to Hear the Voice of God
- How to Never Be Hurt Again
- Taking Charge of Your Emotions
- The Power to Change Today

Audio Series available by Pastor Gregory Dickow

- Financial Freedom: Strategies for a Blessed Life
- How to Pray & Get Results
- Love Thyself
- Mastering Your Emotions
- Redeemed from the Curse
- The Blood Covenant
- Building Your Marriage God's Way

You can order these and many other life-changing materials by calling toll-free 1-888-438-5433.

For more information about Gregory Dickow Ministries and a free product catalog, please visit *www.changinglives.org*